Petals

Hanna Kalo

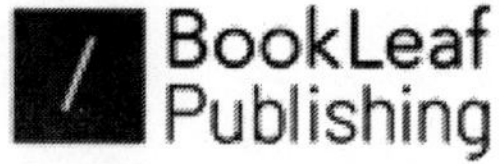
BookLeaf Publishing

Presentation by *BookLeaf Publishing*

Web: www.bookleafpub.com

E-mail: info@bookleafpub.com

ISBN: 9789358736939

First edition 2022

DEDICATION

For Mrs Fay Cookson
who never doubted

PREFACE

the following poems are not for those who wish
to see only the light in the world,
but for those who accept the darkness and make
it their own

the great war of death

(listen to 'I sit beside the fire and think')

The ash coloured sky seems to droop and crush
the life right out of their souls, as the sun comes
up and starts another day in a pointless war
without faith.

as the deafening roar
of the metal animals
breaks the eardrums of all
ash clouds rise to the sky
blocking out the sun's light

and as the war rages on
in both night and day
the human sits still
far away on a small hill

he observes the destruction
of all
unmoving and uncomprehending he sits
and observes it all

bombs fall and explode
and fire burns his skin
tears are in his eyes as he watches families
run for their lives

a little kid stumbles
through the rubble
and collapses onto her knees
grabbing at her throat

from the distance stares the man
as a roof collapses on top of her
cutting her suffering short
and still he sits, observing, unmoving

then the man rises slowly
stepping from stone to stone
he sees a small dark flower
peek out from behind the rubble
of his home

and he falls to his knees
and the flower shines white
in the gloom of everyday
war

the man coughs
and his blood sprays
on the flower's
petals

as his gentle fingers touch the plant
a single black bomb is dropped
and the last aeroplanes dissappear

and for a second, the sky is clear and all is quiet

as the black future drops from the sky
the clouds part and the man
closes his eyes as the black thing
touches the ground

a flash of light
can be felt
and the brightness spreads
like a disease

collapsing
the man shakes on the ground
his fingers craving for the touch
of the flower

but even that
burns up in the
power
of the future

a single petal flutters down
and the man reaches for it
inches from the flower
his finger becomes thin and his skin becomes
grey

they are both incinerated
before they could ever touch
the memory too
dissipitates

and ash drips from the sky
as it cries the blood of those
that died in
vain

for a war that could not be
victoriously won
only ended with the cost of more lives
than it was worth starting it for

and the blood drops to the ground
on which soldiers go ever marching on
they notice the droplets and stop
for a second

turning their faces to the burning sky
and closing their eyes
they whisper a prayer for those that died
before marching on

as if nothing had ever happened
and all was forgotten
never to be mentioned again
and the sky emblazons with the fire of blood

The sky drips blood as the sun droops lower in the sky, ending another day in a pointless war without faith.

Petals fly through the wind

Petals fly through the wind
    I trace the light of the sun
leaves rustle
    with the tip of my finger
trees bow down
    from the heights of heaven
while flowers stand tall
    to the dusts of earth
the screaming beauty from above
    and even below
leaves its cage once more
    where the sun shines from underneath
and storms to freedom
    and the sky never turns dark
never resting in my hair
    I follow the rays
tangling me in thoughts
    until they find me
thoughts of colours
    lying in the depths
of darkness
    of wild flowers
of light
    on a warm summer's eve
thoughts on feelings
    and only one image is captured

which in words cannot be captured
      in the water coloured marks
for they left long ago
      my finger has been drawing
when the wind returned
      a picture of petals
back home to its cage
      of petals...flying.
flying higher than the sun
      higher than even –

The Black Angels of Hiroshima

The whirring, screeching, purring sound of death
Comes ever closer
Black Angels
Fly over Hiroshima
Black wings cut through the blue sky
Burning their way towards us
Plain, strong black wings of angels
Never move, never sway
Their eyes are always watching, observing
All they leave behind them is a deep cut
The sky's wound
Splintering glass, separating us
I look to the sky
One last time
Hoping to see the stars
Before I die,
But to my disbelief
The stars no longer shine
The unmoving wings of the black angels have
covered up all light
Not leaving enough space for one silver slither
of hope
To escape
Before I close my eyes for the last time
I see the black sky

But the last image burned in the back of my
eyelids
Was the white fragments of a line
That split heaven in two
A gift from the black angels of America,
A thin, hopeless border separating heaven from
us.
And Black Angels
Fly over Hiroshima.

A soldier of the war

I do not wish for what most men do,
I only wish to be with my love,
I wish to retire,
for I have seen enough.
I wish to sleep forever,
in her arms,
until the moon climbs higher
and the sun falls lower in the sky
time and time again.
And still I shall not wake,
yet still be
in her arms,
sleeping forever,
for I have seen enough.

some wish for money.
for fame and fortune and health.
some wish for a family.
and still some a secret well kept.
I wish for nigh such as that.

For my dearest and fondest
my most guarded want and need
my one and only wish
is to be with you my love.
To sleep forever in your arms

Dreaming about the wonderful future we would
have.
And the moon
and the sun
may strut across the
starry sky
many a time,
but I would not wake from your arms,
for I have seen enough…

Enough for a lifetime and more,
enough for all the while the sun and moon shall
fight
with the stars.
Enough until they tire and shine no more.
and still, even after the darkness has passed
and light returns with a new sun
once more,
I shall sleep in your comforting arms,
for I have seen enough
I have seen enough.

in the beginning you used to care

you used to care,
in the beginning.
you were shocked, worried, asked me what was
wrong,
every night I cried,
you'd cry with me, or comfort me,
you'd wrap me in a blanket, and watch tv with
me.
you'd hold me tight in your arms, protect me.
but now,
whenever a tear rolls down my face
and drops with a splash,
you don't even have
the curtesy
to pretend that you
Don't hear me.

Forgive me

forgive me,
because tears spill from my eyes
because my breathing is getting shallow
forgive me,
for my eyes cannot dry,
forgive me,
for my knees shake and I am screaming
forgive me,
for even though I know,
even though I feel deep down
you are somewhere better,
I still feel loss.

Forgive me,
but I can't find my way without you
forgive me,
because I want you back.
forgive me,
for if I could,
I would drag you from your mountaintop
where you are enjoying a well-earned rest,
back down to earth
to suffering and pain, just to ease my own…
so forgive me,
it seems I was wrong…
　　　I cannot be happy for you when you are gone.

You talk far into the night

And you still talk,
far into the night
and you laugh
at something he says
i hear your laugh like never before
freer, happier
than when you laugh for me.
it echoes in my ears, sticks in my head
so I fear it will never leave
making me dizzy with confusion;
how can he make you laugh the way
i can't?

i stare out my window,
i should be sleeping,
i said I would be
it was my excuse to leave you two alone,
when you had so much to talk about
and all I could do was nod and smile
and sit in silence by your side.

And still,
you talk far
into the night

mist covers the once white moon
and still, I hear your laugh
for him

the mist leaves,
the moon is yellow with
the early morning's dawn
i should be sleeping,
i said I would be.

but still,
you talk far
into the night.

i stay long by the window
and stare out into open space
the moon disappears too,
leaving me,
will you?

And still,
you talk far
into the dawn.

Therain

splatteringswooshingswiftlysofast
therainfliesthroughthedarknight
asifitneedednotaflashlight
butlightningsoonstrikes
soitsway
ifonlyforamoment
islitup
andonceagain
itcanseewhereitisgoing
beforeallturnsdarkoncemore
andiamleft
wondering
bymyopendoor

9/11

Flames lapping at the sides of the twin icons,
Screams of the traumatized, of the burned,
of the fallen
can be heard.

The sky blackens with soot
as flames hotter than the sun
burn through iron burn through steel
burn through the soul of new york

Falling bodies can be seen,
of those who had jumped
of those who fell
of those who were pushed.

Hundreds of thousands of hands
reaching down towards the safety of land
and desperate eyes searching the heavens
for the slightest breath of air.

The black hand reaches up
ready to suck the air right out of the sky
and the sun hides in shame
as another plane whirrs overhead…

only yesterday

Silent seats
formed around the long face –
d student feeder
quiet whistles
of the wind
fly
from window
to open window

Voiceless ghosts walk about
and as a group nears me
I recognise their voices

We walk silently
our footfalls echoing with soundless quiet
through the dead hall as we near me

I see myself look down onto
me
and frown
as I frowned only yesterday

But then I shrug and sit
next to me
laughing along to a joke
only we know

knew

Only yesterday
we were all here
only yesterday
we were all laughing
only yesterday
we filled the deaf ears
of the dining hall
with the music of our
shrill cries and obnoxious words

Only
yesterday

But now,
the clanging of cutlery and
laughing of my friends,
the words I spoke,
have no more meaning

all that remains of us
is the stories of the wind
reminding the hall
not to forget us

I smile at the memory
and suddenly I can see them all
eating and talking and laughing and walking

I can see the bright lights
smell the food cooking
taste the vinegar on the bland fish
and hear the jokes of my friends
their laugh carrying across the vast space filled
with students
and
me

I turn to my right,
as the laughter dies down
the clanging of cutlery turns
to whispers
and the voices shrill to whistles.

The table's empty.
       I am alone.
            And
            the silent chairs whisper with
            the whistling voice of the wind
                  reminding me
                  of what was
                  what had been
              only yesterday
          but is no more today...

Her eyes were wild

Her eyes were wild beyond belief,
fire swirling in those two
mirrors which showed me her soul
and how dark must a soul be
if the key to simply see it burns in eternal fire?
how dangerous must it be
to reach for that key
within the inferno?
and how dangerous must it be
to guard it every day?
Still I reached and fought the flames,
and although I got burned
along the way
Once I grabbed the key and opened the door to
her soul
the fires stopped burning for me.
Although I still have the marks
where she burned me
She kisses the scars every day
and they don't hurt as much,
as if I never would have tried to reach her
all those years ago
within those wildfire eyes of hers.

purple flowers bloom at night

branches facing downward
broken from their elbows,
from the water
the moon's yellow light
reflects on the sky, and
shines back down
illuminating the darkness of the sun
while the fingers of the old trees
scrape the ground,
they have grown tall
over the past few seconds,
and in the distance mountains climb,
ever lower in the moonset
and flowers bloom at night,
as a face with purple eyes stares back at me
when I lean over the banks
of the river
slipping, sliding in the water-coloured mud
And there I am, dressed all in blue
reflecting myself in purple
all
in this forest, the river's purple
in the river, my dress is purple
in the trees, my sigh is felt
like a wind shifting
branches, higher than they could themselves

and in the river once again,
my eyes stare back
my blue eyes of the purple sky above
stare back at me,
eyes of purple, eyes of hope.

Dip, dip below the pain
(inspired by the art of Isabel Emrich)

the world is
half evil
and her eyes
glisten with tears

the world is
half evil
above the soothing
waves

the world is
half evil
as she dips below
the water's skin

the world is
half evil
but the world is
half good

she looks upwards
through the water's end
through a darkness
with no beginning
to a world that is only

half evil

she sees the trees as they sway
she hears the birds sing
in a world that is only half
evil

but eventually she has
to come up for a breath
and the world turns
real

the world is half evil
loud and pained
her eyes are only able to see
under a blanket of waves

fright

The dark corridors whisper
as the wind whisks by
the shadows deepen
as the moon hides in the blanket of the night
disappears from plain sight
and a scream is heard
in the stillness of the night
cutting through the darkness
of the starless sky
like a cold wind
on a warm summer's night

A siren can be heard
as the ambulance
makes its way down
the deserted street
and the two kids hide
within the blackness of the night
afraid of every stillness
of every shadow
shaking at the slightest movement
from the smallest crow
staring through the window
waiting
for tomorrow.

The Darkness is…

27

A terrifying monster,
A blanket of dust,
A shadow in the corner of my room.
It jumps, it runs,
It flips, it flies,
It crawls, it slides.
Not knowing where it's going,
And not wanting to know where to go.
It creeps out of my room,
It backflips off the stairs,
It makes my heart jump,
It makes my legs run,
It makes my throat scream.
But it takes my screams as cheers,
And my running feet as claps.
I didn't look back,
Just ran and ran.
I never knew what happened
After that moment of terror,
For the light was switched on
And as I looked back,
I saw it was GONE!

The Cat

(special mention to Simon Ireland)

Two green eyes,
Flare up in the dark,
Like torches,
On a cold winter night.

A grey paw,
Slices towards me,
Hardly missing,
Drawing blood.

A long, dark tail,
Flicks in the background,
Like a whip, cracking through the air,
Towards its victim.

It opens its mouth,
White teeth shine in the dark,
Deadly as lightning,
Blinding its victim.

A tremendous roar,
An earthquake starter,
Escapes its mouth;
'Meow?'

Wolves

Howl,
howl tonight
let the wind shine
let the snow scream
let the sun drop
let the rain fly
let the wolf howl
howl, howl
for tonight
nothing will be the same again.
So howl, howl
cry out to the night
for after tonight,
nothing will be the same again.

Had I the time and place

(inspired by the poetry of W. B. Yeats)

Had I the time and place, I'd sing for you,
Had I the heart and soul, I'd paint for you,
Had I the strength and courage, I'd fight for you,
Had I the love and chance, I'd even die for you,
But I can only create, so I write for you.

gone

Unaware of even time itself
you draw black strings
of poesy
from within the depths of my heart

the effect you have on me
is beyond
reality
and through the darkness
of every night

we walk hand in hand
in forests black
and flowers white
til one day we no longer
hold each other
like we used to

for one of us
will be gone
and though the other will
walk on forever more
there will not be you beside me
and now, with you gone

my inspiration has run dry
and I can't even
sleep
through the day.

In shadows dressed she

she dresses in shadows,
but two white stars
that are her eyes
blank white orbs of the night
never could hide
in the darkness
of her

s o u l

Why doth death call to us?

The dreams in life haveth,
Becometh a reality in death.
Those that once loveth and lost,
Will again be found.
That which was destroyeth
Hath been rebuilt.
And doth which thouest loveth,
Will loveth thou back.

ACKNOWLEDGEMENT

Writing this poetry book is a dream come true. Words will never be enough to express my gratitude to all who helped, from the editorial and publishing team, to my ever supportive family and friends. Thank you for always believing in me and encouraging me to follow my dreams.

Endless thanks to all my teachers at Avon House primary school as well, who supported me through my first years of learning English and never doubted I would write. And a special thank you to Fay Cookson who never had a doubt, only support in everything to do with writing.

And of course a massive thank you to all you lovely readers, I write for you and couldn't do this without you!

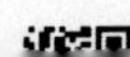